Does God Like to Paint?

Exploring Space with Two Astrophysicists

by Branyon May, Ph.D.
& Alana May, M.S.

ISBN-13: 9781600630934

Library of Congress: 2013933781

Layout and design by
Branyon May & Jim Estabrook

Printed in China

Cover image credit: ESA/Herschel/PACS/SPIRE/J. Fritz, U. Gent; X-ray: ESA/XMM Newton/EPIC/W. Pietsch, MPE

Apologetics Press
230 Landmark Drive
Montgomery, Alabama
36117-2752
www.ApologeticsPress.org

Adapted from Original [NASA/Visible Earth]

Do You Like...*to Paint?*

Everybody loves to paint, especially when there are no pressures or grades and you can paint whatever you want. Finger painting, watercolor, oil painting, and even paint-by-number can stimulate some of your creativity and imagination. Put a pencil, marker, brush, or lump of clay in a young child's hands and you will see all manner of characters, creatures, and creations.

Do You Like...OUTER SPACE?

Everybody loves Outer Space, with its planets, stars, nebulas, and galaxies. If you have ever gazed into the night sky at familiar constellations, seen the rings of Saturn in a telescope, or viewed the brilliance of the Pleiades, then you have also experienced and felt the stunning awe of God's Creation.

Does God Like...*to Paint?*

Does God Like...to Paint? is designed to compare the common childhood tasks of drawing, coloring, painting, and sculpting, with the creativeness of God. As Creator, He demonstrates not only His purposeful design and functional order in the Universe, but His creativity and imagination.

Does God Like... to Draw?

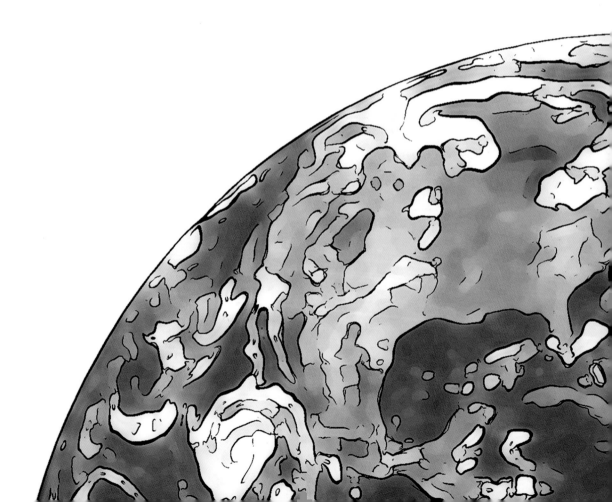

God may not sketch with pencils or pens, but His thoughts and ideas are drawn clearly on His incredible Creation. With masterful etching He creates textured artwork full of contrast and shading.

Adapted from Original
[NASA/Visible Earth]

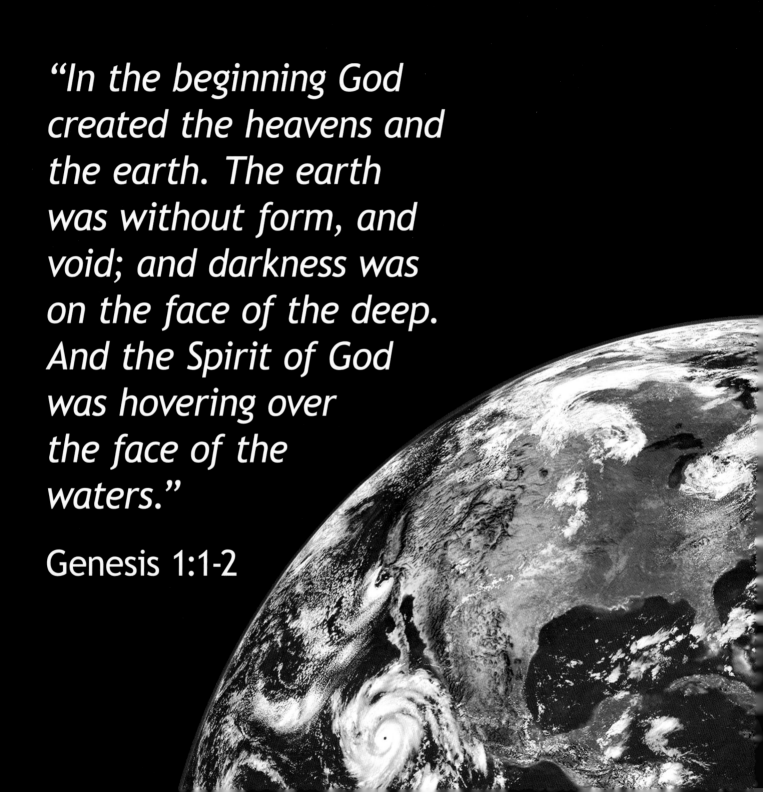

"In the beginning God created the heavens and the earth. The earth was without form, and void; and darkness was on the face of the deep. And the Spirit of God was hovering over the face of the waters."

Genesis 1:1-2

Earth

Our incredible planet has been designed and created as home for mankind. Earth provides all of the vital needs for life to grow and flourish. We have a diversity of lands to live on, an abundance of water, a well-balanced atmosphere, a protective magnetic field, a nearby Moon to influence tides, and a Sun to provide life-sustaining energy and warmth.

NASA/Visible Earth

Does God Like... to Draw?

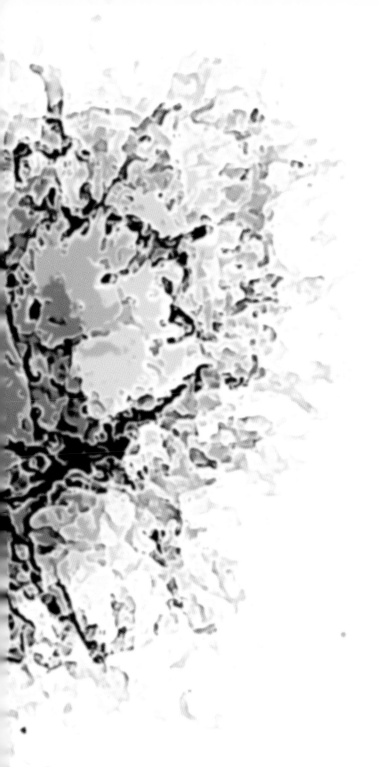

God uses the grandest of mediums as He draws out the Universe using burning stars, glowing clouds of gas, and sparkling galaxies.

"Then God said, 'Let there be lights in the firmament of the heavens to divide the day from the night; and let them be for signs and seasons, and for days and years.'"

Genesis 1:14

Crab Nebula (M1)

This beautifully complex nebula is the remnant of a supernova explosion that has been connected with the historical records from China, Japan, and Arabia of an extremely bright and brief appearance of a star-like object in the sky.

A pulsar has been observed to be near the center of this nebula. As a spinning neutron star, a pulsar emits an observable pulsation of radiation at very short, constant intervals.

(Arizona State University)

Does God Like...
TO COLOR?

Adapted from Original [NASA, ESA, C.R. O'Dell (Vanderbilt University), and M. Meixner, P. McCullough, and G. Bacon (Space Telescope Science Institute)]

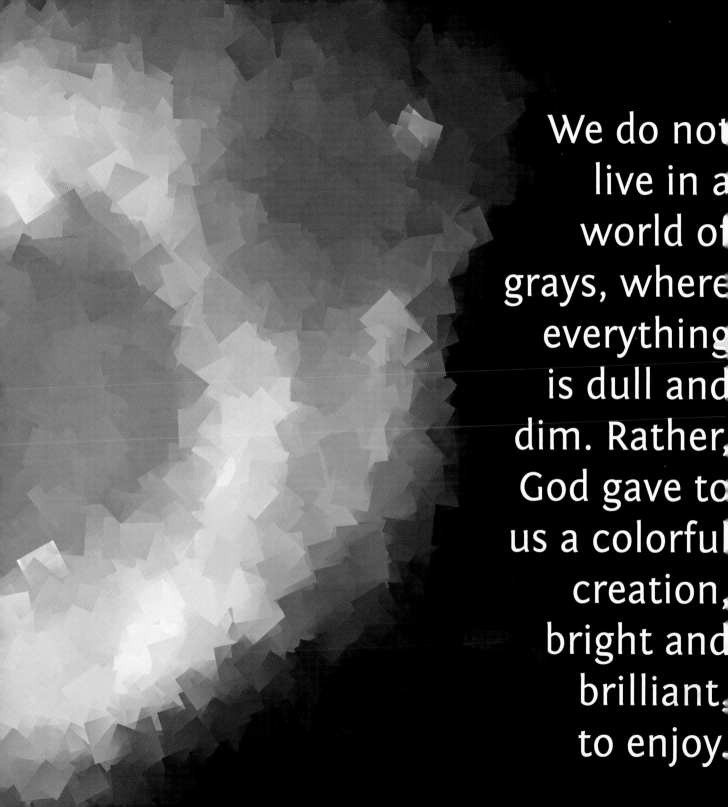

We do not live in a world of grays, where everything is dull and dim. Rather, God gave to us a colorful creation, bright and brilliant, to enjoy.

"By the word of the Lord the heavens were made, and all the host of them by the breath of His mouth."

Psalm 33:6

NASA, ESA, C.R. O'Dell (Vanderbilt University), and M. Meixner, P. McCullough, and G. Bacon (Space Telescope Science Institute)

Helix Nebula

The Helix Nebula (NGC7293) is one of the nearest known planetary nebulas. Its name comes from the concentric, colored rings that surround the central star.

Being relatively close, compared to other planetary nebulas, the Helix Nebula has a large apparent size with a diameter almost as large as the full Moon.

Does God Like...
TO COLOR?

Adapted from Original
[ESA/NASA, ESO and Danny LaCrue]

Every color of
the rainbow,
every shade and
hue, God formed
and fashioned
their beauty
for you.

Tarantula Nebula

The Tarantula Nebula (30 Doradus or NGC2070) is a large emission nebula located in a nearby irregular galaxy called the Large Magellanic Cloud. The Tarantula Nebula encompasses a very large region containing numerous star clusters. The hottest and brightest stars emit large amounts of ultraviolet radiation, which ionize the surrounding gas clouds, producing the visible wisps and arcs.

ESA/NASA, ESO and Danny LaCrue

"He counts the number of the stars; He gives names to all of them. Great is our Lord and abundant in strength; His understanding is infinite."

Psalm 147:4-5

Does God Like...

to Paint?

His paintings do not fit on a canvas and a brush would not fit in His hand, but his murals cover the Earth and the Cosmos is His wonderful mosaic.

"He has made the earth by His power, He has established the world by His wisdom, and has stretched out the heavens at His discretion."

Jeremiah 10:12

The Aurora Borealis

The beautiful dancing lights of the auroras, which are seen often near the North and South Poles, result from God's protective design for Earth. The high energy solar wind that streams outward from the Sun at speeds of 1-2 million miles per hour would have a devastating affect on Earth's life if it were not for the protective cocoon of Earth's magnetic field.

Does God Like...

to Paint?

God is a painter of lights. He uses shadows and shimmers to convey His skill. Instead of mixing colors on a palette, He artfully blends starlight within the winding arms of a spiral galaxy.

"*Thus says the Lord, your Redeemer, and He who formed you from the womb: 'I am the Lord, who makes all things, Who stretches out the heavens all alone, Who spreads abroad the earth by Myself.'*"

Isaiah 44:24

NASA, ESA, S. Beckwith (STScI), and The Hubble Heritage Team STScI /AURA)

The Whirlpool Galaxy (M51)

Spiral galaxies are named for their spiraling and winding arms that often encircle a bright nucleus. Similar to what our own galaxy, the Milky Way, is thought to look like, M51 or the Whirlpool Galaxy has long arms that appear to be wound in a fairly tight pattern. Very regular and ordered in structure, spiral galaxies host dense collections of stars, star clusters, and glowing nebulas.

Does God Like... to Sculpt?

Fashioning and forming, molding and sculpting, God's works are not simply seen in the natural wonders of Earth; they also fill the expanse of the Cosmos.

"For all those things My hand has made and all those things exist,' *says the Lord."*

Isaiah 66:2

Jupiter

The largest planet in our Solar System, Jupiter is primarily made of dense gases held tightly by its enormous gravity. It is also a dynamic planet, with the fastest planetary rotation in our Solar System. It has an active atmosphere swirling with violent storms, and a great many moons bound in orbit around it.

NASA/JPL/University of Arizona

Does God Like...
to Sculpt?

God has sculpted beautiful works such as the celestial spheres of Jupiter, Saturn, and Mars.

Adapted from Original [NASA]

"By faith we understand that the worlds were framed by the word of God, so that the things which are seen were not made of things which are visible."

Hebrews 11:3

Mars

Though Mars has some similarities to Earth, it is also drastically different. Like Earth, Mars has varying geological features, including canyons, mountains, plains, valleys, and deserts. However, the differences are extreme. Mars is a barren, desert-like landscape with no oceans or lakes. The very thin atmosphere, which is about 100 times less dense than Earth's, is a major reason why it has such a different climate and landscape.

NASA

"The heavens declare the glory of God; and the firmament shows His handiwork.... There is no speech nor language where their voice is not heard."

Psalm 19:1,3

The marvelous phenomena of the Universe reflect the glory of the all-powerful God Who made them. The planets, stars, constellations, nebulas, galaxies, and all other amazing features of the Cosmos provide stunning evidence that the God of the Bible exists. The proof is there for all people to see. We can know that He exists!

Having come to a knowledge of God through His natural revelation, we should turn our attention to His special revelation—the Bible. There He reveals more about Himself and what He expects from all of us.

NASA, the Hubble Heritage Team (AURA/STScI) and ESA